Dear Isabella

Pastor Maria Stephens

This book is copyrighted by Veritas Christian Publishing © 2020. All rights reserved. No part of this book may be reproduced, stored, or transmitted in any form, by any means, electronic, mechanical, photocopy, recording, or otherwise, without prior permission from the publisher, except as provided by United States of America copyright law.

Disclaimer: This book addresses the topic of domestic violence, escalating emotional and physical abuse, and pregnancy loss. While the author has gone to great lengths to ensure the subject matter is dealt with in a compassionate and respectful manner, these subjects may trigger or upset some readers. Please use discretion.

Veritas Christian Publishing

822 S. Guignard Dr

Sumter SC 29150

www.veritas.life

Paperback ISBN: 978-1-7359841-0-0

Dedication

Isabella, there will never be enough words to describe my love for you. The deepest wounds and cracks within my mind and soul have become the places that the wildflowers now grow.

To my husband, Gerald Stephens, for standing by me and helping me realize that incredible men still exist.

To my spiritual parents, Bishop Walter & Pastor Monica McLeod, for never giving up on me and speaking to the God given potential I had hidden from the world.

Dedicated to the victims and lives lost to domestic violence.

Table of Contents

Introduction 1

Chapter 1 2

Chapter 2 4

Chapter 3 6

Chapter 4 10

Chapter 5: One Year after Isabella's Arrival 12

Chapter 6: Till Death Do Us Part 14

Chapter 7: The Safe House 17

Chapter 8: Rescued 20

Chapter 9: Hidden 23

Epilogue: October: Isabella's Story 25

Introduction

For ten years, my first marriage was anything but bliss. I spent many days in frantic fear, trying desperately to keep the peace as violence ripped through my self-esteem, my marriage, and the walls of my home. Domestic violence was a slogan I saw on posters hanging in the bathrooms. I didn't understand that it was actually happening to me.

I adapted to the domestic violence as it began with jealousy and control in minor ways. However, these behaviors worsened over time. In my own naivety, I believed that this was normal, and I usually accepted blame for his outbursts. I suffered in silence until, one day, I decided to write a journal expressing and releasing my fears—fears I felt I just couldn't share with anyone else. I was so afraid that my abuser would find my journal. So this story begins with my journal writing to my daughter; I hid the journal in the wall of a well in my front yard. At the time, I had no intentions of sharing these graphic scenes with her. I was so excited about her expected arrival and wanted to let her know.

The letters eventually shift to the reader as I tell the story of domestic violence following Isabella's birth. My goal is to reach the daughters of those who may be encountering domestic violence in hopes that they will read these entries and seek help. If it were not for someone's testimony, I wouldn't have broken free from abuse and come out on the other side, advocating through Isabella's story. One day, I could finally reach through the walls of my own inner well, by the grace of God, to retrieve those personal, hidden parts of me that I was once ashamed of, I brought them into the light as a testimony of overcoming! May the words on each page be received and bring awareness to the silent killer of domestic violence.

Chapter 1

Dear Isabella,

I don't know how to put into words how excited I am and terrified to know I am carrying life again. You are a complete surprise, but I believe you will be a missing piece needed in my world. Your brother Jo is two years old; he also came unexpectedly, but he has forever changed me from a teenage girl to a mother. I sometimes still try to connect to that role and not merely carry the title. I don't know what moms are supposed to feel, but I know I have all kinds of emotions coursing through me. Movies and television have given me the idea of that framed, cookie-cutter image that the world shows as motherhood. So far I feel as if I don't fit into any of those molds. If anything, I envy their lives as I fantasize about what it must be like to feel loved, honored, and cherished and to have a stable home, safe and functional and full of joy, peace, and acceptance.

I guess what I'm trying to say is I carry the name "Mom," but my circumstances and the battles I face with your dad result in feelings of unworthiness to carry the name and position of mother. The constant cycle of pulling me in and tossing me aside only confirms my lack of worth in my own eyes. I do the best I can with your brother. I love him. I play outside with him as he hunts for bad guys and snakes. I run with him, throw the ball to him, push him on the swing, protect him, and so completely love his sweet and gentle spirit. When your dad is at work and it is just the two of us, I feel most at home. For the first time in my life, the name "Mother" gives me purpose, a home I belong to. As a mom, I have a place where I am free to love, where I am needed by someone who simply wants me for me, just as I am.

That feeling of a warm, safe home doesn't last long. The storm blows into the house around five o'clock each day when he comes home. An intense fear of the unknown enters the room. It can come in like a gentle misty rain, but at some point, without warning, a tornado can quickly spin off from the rain clouds. Your dad loves me, at least that's what he tells me. He often puts his hands around my neck as he spits out his venom. That venom painfully absorbs into my skin, but I try to wash it off and accept that I am to blame for his anger. If I had only done this or that, or I should have known this, or I should not be doing that. I tell myself I will eventually get it right, so I accept the blame. I make sure to correct it to prove to him I love him and will not make those mistakes again. So far, I cannot seem to get it right, and I feel like a failure for causing so much anger in him. I cannot seem to figure out what he really wants. He says it's because I am stupid and there must be something wrong with my brain to keep screwing up. He thinks I do it on purpose to undermine him. He tells me all the time he has a lot more experience with street life than I do, so he knows (expletive) when he sees it. Communicating with him is so burdensome. I never know what will set him off. He somehow misinterprets everything I say into something far-fetched that I didn't mean at all.

I am scared to tell him I am pregnant. I do not know if he will be delighted or angry with me. I will wait until tomorrow to say anything about the pregnancy because we are having a peaceful day. Out of caution, I will wait until later just in case he isn't thrilled to have a child with someone like me.

Chapter 2

Dear Isabella,

I do not know the purpose of writing to you as if you were my personal diary, but maybe, one day, you will reflect on these words, or maybe I can use reflect on my own words. On the other hand, I might not want you to discover these intimate thoughts. Maybe one day, I will want to burn every page, or maybe one day, you will read this in remembrance of a mother who couldn't wait to share everything with her first daughter, her best friend. Either way, it feels good to begin this bond with you before I even get to meet you. I dream of you. I see a brown-eyed, curly brown-haired Spanish beauty with your mom's single dimple resting on your cheek, olive skin, and a smile that melts the hardest of hearts. I have not even confirmed whether you are a girl or a boy; I have only taken a pregnancy test and dreamed you are a girl.

I told your dad about you yesterday, and he was so happy, he picked me up and spun me around. He has been treating me like a delicate flower, getting me whatever I am craving, mainly salt-and-vinegar chips.

I went to the doctor today for your first visit. They confirmed a positive pregnancy test. I heard your heartbeat for the first time, the sweetest sound, and had butterflies as if I fell in love with you all over again! A delicate beat, yet fast and strong. The midwife said a beat that rapid could indicate a girl. However, she confessed that was an old wives' tale. They determined I was about ten weeks and two days pregnant. They drew my blood, and genetic testing will determine if you are the girl I know I've been blessed with. However, I have to wait a week or two for those results. I am to come back in three weeks for an ultrasound.

I get to peek in a window as they measure for a more accurate due date. I am counting down the days. Your dad has been so nice to me since I told him about you; he even insisted I reapply for college and finish my degree after I said I was determined to reach my goal. He was overly kind to me about all my dreams and desires.

So I registered for school, and I begin classes tomorrow. I will be taking evening classes so that your dad can sit with Jo while I go to school. My major is criminal justice because I have always had a huge passion for that field. My dream has always been to become an officer or an investigator. I believe you were exactly what I said: a missing puzzle piece that I needed. Things appear normal and calm, and this peace is nice. For now, I am packing my books and preparing for school tomorrow, I love you, sweet girl. I can't wait to tell you how it went.

Chapter 3

Dear Isabella,

It's been a few days since I wrote. I couldn't wait to share how my first day of school went, but I have just found the courage to even write because everything I imagined has completely been destroyed, assassinated.

I went to class: first, my English class followed my criminal justice class. I was only one of four females in the class. I was excited to be doing something to better myself. My fear lingered that your dad might not like the dynamics of the classroom since the majority were males. But I brushed away the thought and refocused on my studies. The first lesson was on the topic of police officers and their job-related stress. We watched a video of an officer sitting on the courthouse steps with a gun to his head. He suffered from PTSD. A negotiator, desperate to stop the suicide attempt, was pleading with him and reminding the officer of his value and purpose.

The warmth of my tears suddenly splashed onto my desktop. I was reminded of my grandfather, an officer, who had taken his life. I was caught off guard by my grief. I've never handled hurt or grief well. I tend to just keep moving, fearing I will choke on the crushing of my heart within my chest. I quickly realized I needed to go to the restroom to pull it together before I watched another minute of this video. I didn't want to be on public display or seen as someone emotionally unstable or weak.

Your dad has conditioned my response to grief. A single tear from my eyes was like a taunt to him. He invited himself to a fight that I did not know I was attending after a single tear, no matter the cause. It was almost as if my tears said to him, "Hey, screw you, buddy."

So when the tears simply fell from my face without any control, I was embarrassed. As I went back to class, my instructor was waiting outside. He was young and appropriately named. Mr. Grace had precisely that: tons of grace and compassion. He asked if I was okay. I told him why I was struggling to watch the video in class, and he said he had a feeling something triggered me. So he wanted to meet me at the door to let me know I could sit in the computer lab until the video ended. He excused me for the next half hour. He was so understanding and gracious. After thirty minutes, I returned to class and continued with a group activity, then class dismissed.

When your dad arrived to pick me up, I felt sick to my stomach. I thought it was pregnancy symptoms, but this feeling was all too familiar. It was fear, shaking in my gut. Mr. Grace walked by as I entered the car. He smiled, waved and said he would see me next week. I immediately feared how your dad would respond to the kindness of the teacher. Last time a male was nice to me, your dad accused me of sleeping with that man, and we argued for hours. The majority of that time was his psychological breakdown of my every statement.

He had the ability to make me lie by twisting my statements and confusing me so much that I did not know what to say or how to say it. No matter what I said, it was never the right thing. My words were always beaten like a tortured stray. With these thoughts loudly clamoring in my head, we exited the parking lot. His energy angrily shifted gears and aggressively accelerated. The rainbow–and–butterfly feelings that I had danced with since announcing this pregnancy flew out the car window into traffic. In its place, a swarm of hornets and fire swirled in. Anger radiated from his pierced lips, his sharp demeanor warning me of what was to come.

I asked, "Is everything okay?"

He said, "I don't know. Is it?"

"What are you talking about?"

He replied, "Don't play your (expletive) games with me." I honestly didn't know why he was so furious. "How many dudes are in your class?"

I told him I was not sure of the exact number, but there were more men than women in the class. He said, "You (expletive) liar. I went to your class but where the (expletive) were you?" I tried explaining what happened, and he began recklessly speeding as he said he would sideswipe the car just the right way and take us out if I didn't start telling the truth.

But I *was* telling the truth; he just would not listen. He was so paranoid and convinced I was in the bathroom with another man even though I told him I was in the computer lab. He said that was a (expletive) lie because he went into the class while I was in the bathroom and asked my teacher where I was. Apparently, the teacher was put off by his aggressive questioning, and he told your dad that he needed to leave. All the men rose from their seats, and your dad said, "Well, (expletive) y'all." I was mortified! I quickly realized why the teacher met me in the hallway after I went to the restroom. I wanted to disappear at the idea of what the others were probably thinking. I didn't believe I could ever go back there again. The tears came pouring out, not from sadness but from anger.

He continued to scream at me and sped down a dirt road and jumped this huge hill. Jo was in the back seat, sleeping through all the madness until the car jumped the hill at a high speed. He woke up crying. At that moment, I didn't matter anymore. I was focused on ending the fight and bringing the situation to a quick resolution for Jo's safety. I told him I was sorry and assured him my story was true and that he didn't deserve to be treated that way by my professor. I said whatever I could to calm him down. The words coming out of my mouth were taking a part of me with them as they rolled off my lips. But I had to tell him what he wanted to hear.

We pulled into the driveway and entered the house. He snatched my book bag from me and said he didn't believe me "Just to make sure you aren't full of (expletive), let me end this (expletive) right now." He took out my school books and ripped them to pieces like a lion tearing into its prey. He shredded my dreams apart. As each page ripped, it was as if a reflection of my identity were being torn, one page at a time. He then tossed each piece aside, not even worthy putting them into a wastebasket.

This letter to you is the only safe place I can have a voice without fear or intimidation. I realize now that writing to you is now putting me at risk of his discovery of my written words and devouring me even more. For now, I will sign off and say I love you. I don't think it is safe to continue these secret journal entries. I have nowhere to hide them that he won't find them. I need to focus on keeping the peace and helping him as much as I can because I don't want you welcomed into a home full of chaos and tension. I can't wait to see you on the ultrasound in thirteen days, love!

Chapter 4

Dear Isabella,

It's been a week since I wrote to you last. I know I said I was not going to write anymore. However, I miss writing to you, and I'm so alone without anyone to share the innermost parts of my heart and soul

I'm no longer in school after our blowout about all the men in my class. Besides, he destroyed all my books. He said I could return to school only if I majored in something that was more for a woman, like nursing school. It would be a long journey to even be accepted into the nursing program; only the academically advanced get in. I barely know how to do basic math, I don't feel that intelligent, and I feel as if school is now a fantasy, something out of my reach. However, all I can do is try. I have to start at the beginning with basic math, reading, and English classes. That alone will take two years to complete. I will need those classes simply to begin college level classes. That alone will make me want to quit before I begin, but I know that the only way to get there is to at least begin. In the spring, three months from now, I plan to register again for classes that are more agreeable to your dad. By then, I should be closer to your estimated due date of April 23. If you come that day, your brother and you will share a birthday.

Later That Day

Something terrible has happened. My sweet girl, please tell me you are okay. The one place you should be safe. Please be okay! I'm in so much pain: physically, emotionally, and mentally. I didn't hear your dad calling my name as my focus was locked on the conversation on the TV show I was watching. I was not paying any attention to him. I didn't ignore him intentionally; I was not trying to disrespect him by showing more interest in the television show. I honestly didn't hear him.

When he snatched my feather pillow out from under my head and angrily hurled it into my stomach with every bit of strength he had, I was completely unaware of what or why he was so mad. Oh my sweet girl, I'm so sorry! I should have been paying attention and noticed he was about to attack. I should have done a better job of protecting you. The cry of pain that came from within didn't help either. He dragged me by the hair into my bedroom as I screamed. The moment he yelled, "Maybe next time you'll listen when I'm calling you!" was the only reason I knew why he snapped. I'm so scared.

He left. I quickly ran to the well to get my journal. Now I'm afraid to move. I am going to rest and hope this pain in my stomach goes away. Please be okay. I won't move the rest of the day to ensure you are okay. We will get through this together. I must hurry and hide this journal back in the well before he returns. I definitely do not want to be the cause of another backlash from him.

I will rest now. Besides, tomorrow I get to meet you on the big screen and hear the gentle drum beat of your heart. Your life flowing through my veins and mine into yours is a beautiful thought. I'm excited to see just how big you are at thirteen weeks.

Chapter 5
One Year after Isabella's Arrival

Dear Reader,

I did continue with school and took one or two classes a semester for five years just to finish the classes needed to apply for nursing school. My home environment remained in chaos; however, I persevered despite the abuse. I managed to ears A's and B's in every class I took, except for one class. I was told I couldn't leave the house the night of my final exam, which hurt my grade.

The jealousy only grew worse over the years. I did what I could just to keep the peace, however, he took that as a challenge. He effectively attacked every insecurity to assure his control over me.

The year after Isabella's birthdate, I was pregnant again. Due to what I faced during my pregnancy with Isabella, I knew I didn't want to submit another one of my children to the abuse I endured. So I packed my bags and moved in with my parents. Leaving was the bravest thing I ever did. He was so angry at first, but when he realized he couldn't abuse me without going through my parents, he began to change his ways. (My father scared him.) He began going to church and working on his anger issues by getting counseling. Living with my parents was a nice, safe place to retreat, but I couldn't help but miss home, as dysfunctional as it was. It was still a part of what I knew. I tried to focus on all the bad so I wouldn't miss the hell I had finally escaped from.

As weeks turned into months, I noticed consistency in his behavior, which gave me hope that restoration was possible. The more I went to church with him, the more I desired to forgive him. He asked me to come home for dinner, so I did. He had our home and bedroom refurnished with newer and better furniture than what we have ever had. We were no longer in the home with the well but in another place in the country. It felt like a home: warm and inviting. Just as inviting were his smiles and the love, affection, kindness, and apologies he showered me with, along with promises he would never again mistreat me. Then he got down on one knee with a box in one hand and my hand in his. He cried as asked me to be his wife. I accepted. I was only a couple of weeks away from my due date, so we decided to marry at the courthouse. I was huge and pregnant when we said, "I do." Until we said our vows, he was upholding his promises and even consistently treated me with kindness. However, the moment we exchanged our vows was the moment I would later live to regret.

Chapter 6
Till Death Do Us Part

Dear Reader,

Soon after the marriage ceremony, hidden within the shadows of a smooth talker, lurked something darker than what I ever faced. The marriage gave him confidence that he had an advantage over me. He was the provider, and I was completely financially dependent on him. I could not work due to a medical classification as a high risk pregnancy.

I knew the darkness had returned as the day he entered the house half drunk and full of cocaine. As he lit up a huge marijuana cigarette, I could not believe he was in the house with pot, smoking away. We had never smoked inside our home—ever! Especially since immature lungs were still in the home and developing in my womb. He began puffing away and blew it in my face. I told him to please take it outside. He replied, "This is my house, and I can do what I want when I want!"

I don't know what happened within me, but I became ultra-protective. I stood my ground and asked him "Will you take the joint outside? I don't want it around the kids." He chuckled and for the first time in a long time, he laughed with that familiar, sarcastic passive-aggressiveness. His eyes went dark as if he were an empty vessel. He had once again the person he promised to never become. In fact, he didn't become that person he said he would never be again; he became something darker, something even worse. I did not know how dark he had become until I made the mistake of standing up for myself that night.

When I told him for the third time to go outside and smoke his joint, he laughed again, and said "(expletive) you," as he proceeded to walk past me. Like a knee jerks when an anvil hammer hits that spot, my reflex reaction happened so quickly I wasn't even afraid until the act was done. I snatched the joint out of his mouth and waddled my thirty-eight-week pregnant behind toward the bathroom. As he jumped up, he snarled and said, "You ain't that stupid." I almost hesitated in fear, but I was motivated to show him just how "stupid" I was. I wanted him to know I wasn't going to accept his former ways or behavior. I entered the bathroom and tossed the joint in the toilet, knowing there was no going back. He entered the bathroom and said, "Where is it?"

I said "Where do you think?" He looked puzzled and even hesitated reacting because he really didn't believe I would have the courage to do what I did. I moved back so he could see for himself. When he spotted it, I reached over him and flushed the toilet. I walked away. He followed me, screaming profanities and insults as we entered the kitchen. I told him, "If you don't calm down, I am going to have to leave."

He laughed and said, "You're my (expletive) wife now, and you aren't going anywhere." As I turned to walk away, he swooped down and grabbed both of my ankles. I lost my balance and fell belly first at thirty-eight-weeks pregnant onto the hard kitchen floor, with no time to catch my fall. My pregnant belly crashed so hard onto the floor that a shock like lightning coursed through my body. I thought I broke my back. I was face down on the floor in shock, pain, and absolute distress. I couldn't even make sense of his psychotic rantings. When the ringing in my ears stopped, I blacked out.

I regained consciousness as he said, "That's what you (expletive) get for trying to leave. The only way you are leaving here is in a body bag. I know you hear me you piece of (expletive)!" His face pressed against my ear as his jaws clenched, his words forced out. Then he snatched my hair and said, "Get the (expletive) up, stop playin' me, stop faking like something is wrong with you. You'd better hope nothing is wrong with my baby."

I blacked out again. I woke up and lifted my head, the red stain mural of my face imprinted on the floor. Delirious, I thought that red was never a flattering color for me. I again lost consciousness, then opened my eyes to see him sitting in the chair, reclining, watching pornography. He looked over at me and said, "What are you staring at?" He began praising the way the women on the video looked and comparing me to them by saying what they have that I don't. He talked about how gross I looked to him. He demanded that I watch TV as he talked about the many ways the women in the porn movie turned him on as he shamed my body. He even stated his disgust with my pregnant belly by pointing out my stretch marks.

The physical pain was becoming unbearable. I sat up, and he screamed, "You'd better not get up!" I was emotionally overwhelmed. The salt of my tears stung, burning like a trail of fire as they fell past my busted lip into the surrounding pool of blood. I had lost track of how long I had been on the floor. What I did know was there my unborn son and I might possibly die that night. He coldly stated, "Stop that crying. You caused this by taking my smoke and trying to leave me.

I pleaded weakly, "I need to go to the hospital. I am having contractions. I think I'm in labor."

He continued watching porn and said, "Have that baby on the floor for all I care, but you ain't going anywhere."

I began to choke and throw up from the pain and stress. "I need some water."

He got up and asked, "You need water?" He filled up a tea pitcher, then stood over me as I lay on the floor. He tilted his head sideways with a sarcastic glare. "You want water?" I nodded yes and reached up, then he dumped the pitcher of cold water over my head. "Here's your water (expletive)." He threw the pitcher at me and went back to watching his porn. I blacked out again for an unknown amount of time until I woke to him dragging me to the bedroom where he then raped me violently.

Chapter 7

The Safe House

Dear Reader,

I never spoke about what happened that night. I had my son a few days after that traumatic night. As usual, the apologetic man stood before me. It was not so much that I believed him, but a switch within myself went off. It had been off since we lived at the house by the well. That switch ignited life inside my bones, a pulsating beat that reminded me that I was alive. But it was now dead within me. A part of me was sealed up like a vaulted well. I was breathing with a heartbeat. I loved my children, lived to provide, and protect them the way I knew how. However, the pieces of me that once shined brightly were now shadowed. I withdrew from my family but continued with school at night working toward a degree. I didn't believe I would ever achieve it; he would probably try to ruin that, too, but I went anyway. The classes would later be what kept my head above water as I was losing my will to live.

I came home one day from the grocery store and pulled into the yard. He strolled up with a puppy. *Another addition to our dysfunctional family.* He told me I could name him, so I called him Pancho. I never had my own pup, and I soon began to find that he was therapeutic for me. Pancho would climb in my lap and stay with me all the time. His closeness and desire to be near me without any expectation helped me start to come alive again. He was my little peacemaker. I used to feel as if he shouldn't be my dog because he constantly shook. I thought he probably needed a doggy Valium from the constant stress.

But the vet told me this was actually his way of wagging his tail to express joy. His tail was partially paralyzed, so his joy came from within, and his shivering expressed it. If he was overjoyed, his whole body would shake. I giggled for the first time in months at Pancho. When I came home from the grocery store, he was so thrilled his whole body shook back and forth. Instead of a wagging tail, he was wagging his whole body with his tongue hanging out. I laughed so hard that I couldn't stop. I hadn't laughed in so long that the endorphins from it almost made me high, and I couldn't contain it.

He heard me, and in his insecurities, he thought I was laughing at him. I was trying to tell him why I was laughing, but I couldn't stop laughing long enough to put sentences together. All I could do was point at Pancho and laugh. He began to walk down the steps, and Pancho always fled from him. But in the excitement, Pancho didn't notice him until his foot stomped down the steps. Pancho froze as if he didn't know which direction to go. At that moment, Pancho ran up the steps in fear, trying to rush to the back door. In the process, he rolled between my husband's feet, and he fell. I immediately stopped laughing because I didn't want to be vulnerable to any feelings of joy because of his impulsive anger.

He reached out before Pancho could get by, and as I ran toward them, I screamed, "No!" at the top of my lungs. He dropkicked my dog like a football, up so high into the air that all I heard was my heart break when my dog hit the ground. I cried so hard as I held the lifeless Pancho in my hands. He was still just a pup, and he didn't deserve what happened.

He went to go shower, and I grabbed my children and quickly devised an escape, knowing if he caught me I would be the next one who would suffer the consequences. I got in the car, and as soon as I cranked it, he ran out the house so fast, I punched the accelerator. My adrenaline was pumping, as my will to escape alive rushed through my veins. He ran and jumped on the hood and tried diving in the sunroof. I swerved the car, and he rolled off the side.

I sped away and ended up in another town where I found a safe house for women fleeing abuse. I remained there, got a job and began taking steps toward my independence. However, after eight months, he returned from a Christian rehabilitation place in another state. We began co-parenting, and he got visitation but only at my aunt's house.

He soon found an area of weakness and talked me into mending our family. He appeared to be putting forth the effort and was even trying to build relationships with my immediate family, which had never happened. My family, at this point, didn't know the extent of the abuse in the ways I truly experienced it. I had never found the courage to tell them of those shameful places of abuse. It was embarrassing, and I honestly didn't know how to put it into words. He offered to take me to his hometown halfway across the country. He showed me the beautiful places in God's country, as he called it. I moved there with him

After barely a year there, I endured the worst kinds of abuse and rape. I packed my luggage in the middle of the day, and at almost nine months pregnant with my third son, I made the long thousand-mile drive back home. I had nowhere to go because, at that time, my parents were temporarily moving out of town to help her brother and sister-in-law. I took what little money I had and found a rental. I knew I would only be able to afford one month of rent, which was long enough for me to give birth, recover, and figure out my next move. But when I went into labor, he showed up. I had to have a C-section. The surgery would require more time for me to heal, and out of options and in desperation, I allowed him back one last time. I would stay for four more years before I finally decided to walk out and never, ever look back.

Chapter 8
Rescued

Dear Reader,

For the next four years, I continued with college and finally reached my goal. I couldn't believe after all I faced I actually completed every class needed to apply for nursing school, including every prerequisite: all my electives, sciences, math, English classes and even computer class passed with As and Bs. My accomplishments felt almost surreal, and the most rewarding part was that this was mine, and no one could take it from me.

The day came to receive acceptance letters. I checked my mail, and there sat my letter of denial or acceptance. Only seventy-five out of the hundreds that applied would be chosen. I was scared to open the letter but finally slit the envelope open. The first sentence broke through me like a bullet from a gun.

I was not accepted. I cried and completely lost all hope. I couldn't believe that after all I went through, it was over. I would not be allowed to reapply for another year. I was depressed for three days. I didn't get out the bed and was ready to just give up. I had prayed so diligently and asked God to please show up and make a way even though it seemed as if there was no way. I thought, *If you did it for Moses, do you love me that much? Would you part the seas for me to escape the hands of the enemy?* I didn't understand what I prayed for. I just sensed it, a pleading to be free from it all.

The phone rang almost immediately. My school advisor asked why I hadn't turned in my packet. I asked, "What packet?" She told me that all students who were accepted into the program had to return the packet by the due date stamped inside. I told her I hadn't been chosen according to the letter I received. She said that must have been a mistake because I was chosen. "Are you willing to accept your spot?"

I can only describe that moment as unbelievable joy from within. I knew without question, a way was made when it seemed as if there was no way. The sea was parted for me to go straight through, and when I finally reached the other side, I would be free, and the enemy that chased me would not catch me as long as I kept pushing forward. I began my journey into full-time nursing school. It was complicated, considering the circumstances I faced and managing a busy household of little ones. However, I did it. I learned how to survive and persevere despite the circumstances working overtime to hold me back. I passed my first semester.

On the day of my final exams, I packed up my broken pieces, my children, and the clothes on our backs and fled. I never looked back; I just focused on the road ahead. I didn't have much, but I had my life, my children, and faith. I didn't care what I lacked. I trusted the promise God showed me: that he would always make a way. It would be up to me to put my faith in action and move forward when he cleared a path for me. I ran toward the promised land.

Today, I write this as a free woman. The enemy never caught me again. Oh, he tried. He stalked me and even assaulted me, but someone always showed up before it went too far. He couldn't get to me, no matter how much he tried. I kept pushing forward. Even when the courts failed to give me protection orders or when the charges against him were lowered, I never gave in, I fought for my life again.

Blessings came to me that aided me in the journey. An angel of a woman came to me, and she told me God spoke to her in a dream that she was to give me what I needed to get those freedom papers:

my divorce. She wouldn't take no for an answer. I didn't want her to be out fifteen hundred dollars. But she said it was an investment and told me to pay it forward. It took three years of battles in court, but I walked away a free woman with full custody and a new beginning. God fulfilled another promise. He makes all things work together for good as we just keep moving forward.

Today, I continue to pay it forward as my God sent me a new husband. We pursue God's will in our lives and for others while serving as pastors under the leadership of our spiritual parents. They saw past our circumstances and into our hearts. They saw the potential and encouraged us toward greatness. My husband and I are now family life pastors, and we share a son together and all four of my children. My husband has branded them in his heart as his own as well. Never give up. No matter what it looks like, never lay down to die, fight, and keep moving forward. Even with just a little faith, mountains will move. There is nowhere you can go that God won't show up and rescue you. You just have to be willing to chase after him, no matter what, without looking back. I am no longer a slave to fear. I am a living, breathing, wild flower that dances in the wind and shines in his light.

Chapter 9
Hidden

Dear sweet Isabella,

For so long, I lived in survival mode, numb to the trauma. Through incredible men and women of God, I could begin true restoration and healing. When I went to the well, hidden within the cracked walls of my soul, I found the secret place where you were hidden. Despite the trauma of it all, I was convinced to keep going and never think about it again. Regretfully, I did that. I wrote the last letter to you fifteen years ago and said I couldn't wait to see you on the big screen. My letters then stopped because a few hours after the last letter, something terrible happened. I couldn't accept the grief, so I tore out the letter and put it at the end of this book. Then I hid it inside the walls of the well.

One day, as I began my journey toward healing, I went back to the house with the well. I was curious if my journal was still hidden there after I dreamed about revisiting the well. I didn't want to go to the property because I had moved on and had no desire to look back. However, I have come to trust God enough to know that he wanted to reveal something to me. Sometimes we need to look back, not to go backward but to collect broken pieces as God mends us. We can't move forward into our greatest potential until we can look back and stare the wolf in the eye.

I went at night, on my way home from work, under a bright full moon. When I arrived, I pulled into the driveway, and the house of hell was gone! I thought it was just that dark and I couldn't see, so I turned my bright lights on. But it was no longer standing. Only the white raised cement foundation remained where that house once stood. I began to laugh. I cried and laughed. I cried, laughed, and screamed. In that moment of hysteria, peace filled my car. The Holy Spirit stirred within me and said to me, "The house may fall, but what remains is hope to rebuild until your dream house is complete. You've had many walls destroyed. Your frame beaten, bruised, and damaged. The house that stood here was not the home I designed for you. You've lived in many houses, you've even been homeless, but this foundation still stands. So rise up, my child, get out the car, reach inside that well, and release what you find to me."

When I reached in and faced my grief, I released it to God. As I'm releasing it now for the world to hear, may Isabella's story become a testimony that inspires others to reach into the walls of their wells to release whatever is hidden.

Epilogue
October: Isabella's Story

The smell of wet dirt and mildew from the fallen leaves in their resting place stenches the crisp air. This smell used to excite me as a child as I jumped into the leaf piles, laughing. Innocent, young, carefree, free-spirited—that is what every October smelled like to me. Even as I grew older, I loved awakening that childlike spirit by allowing seasonal aromas to trigger those emotional connections. However, I knew that after today, that smell would no longer excite me but instead rob part of me and bring forth grief, a haunting one should never endure.

The engine is loud, but my heart beats louder. I struggle to catch my breath as it races with my heart. It feels as if I've been raped again, but this time I am being forced to comply with that which doesn't involve sexual but yet unthinkable acts.

The oak tree hovering over the abandoned graveyard appears to be mourning. The heavy branches that have held up many seasons are stretched downward as one's arms do when slouching down from carrying an unspoken sadness. The streaks and glistening trails of tears reflect the tree sap that flows down the trunk toward the rooted feet of its mount. The chain-link fence around the graveyard is painted with rust. The entry gate portrays the neglect in its disintegrated, dilapidated appearance, weathered and battered from the harsh elements of nature. The thick layers of many Octobers rest under that mourning oak tree and block the swinging of the gate as if hesitating to welcome anyone inside. He decided to conceal his act of violence with a white sock wrapped around the specimen cup this time. He usually diverts blame, and mental manipulation is his white sock, but this time, he can't use words for what I am holding in my trembling hands.

I convince myself to do what needs to be done to protect her from any further mishandling than she has already suffered while inside my womb for her thirteen weeks of life. Completely traumatized and in shock, all I feel is the coldness from the specimen cup that stayed at the bottom of the refrigerator where he placed her for days as I mourned and grieved. I imagine the white sock around the specimen cup she rests in is like a blanket to comfort her. The thunder cracks, echoing my heart as it beats one last time as my emotions and everything about me dies within. The rain competes with my tears, the agony to press on and find a resting place for my daughter screams out loud into the storm. As the tornado spins toward me, fierce, ready to destroy, he comes roaring toward me as his boot digs into the decaying leaves, penetrating the soil. His impatient stammer and frustration rips the Earth open, a small, dark hole to bury his guilt, concealing his destruction with dirt as he storms off like a tornado diminishing into the sky.

I hide her in the hidden place that his boot imprinted in my heart and into the ground. The cold soggy mud slides away from my hands and falls heavily onto the clean white sock. As the white turns to filth, every layer of dirt placed on top of innocence is a part of me that I bury with her. With the last pat on the soil, I silently say a prayer. *My precious jewel. I am sorry. Forgive me! You did not deserve to have your life taken! God, I am sorry, forgive me! I know you must be angry at all that is taking place. Please, tell me she is with you! Tell her I love her. I hope to meet her one day. Until then, will you tell her everything about me? Please be with me. I am not okay right now! The pain is more than I can handle! Just make it stop*! I rise to my feet and slowly walk away. The truck pulls away. The tears flow, and as I wipe them away, they sting my cheek. The street sign at the end of the dirt road is called Haven Road. It didn't mean anything at that moment. All I could see was the dirt under my nails, and from that moment, October became a different season in my heart.

In loving memory of my daughter Isabella Maria, who continues to break the silence through me as I presently advocate for women and children who have been affected or are currently affected by domestic violence. Isabella Maria died after thirteen weeks in my womb. She passed away shortly after my abuser struck a powerful blow to my stomach. It took me many years to revisit the trauma of losing my one and only daughter. I was a victim of domestic violence for ten years and have been set free from that captivity for eight years now. If you would like to hear my testimony and Isabella's story in full, please go to the following link. Share it with anyone who may be encouraged by it. https://youtu.be/GIVmDVKLiWM

www.ingramcontent.com/pod-product-compliance
Lightning Source LLC
Chambersburg PA
CBHW062207100526
44589CB00014B/2005